FOREWORD

Letter to Mom
by Elizabeth Hansen Kincaid

Dear Mom:

It's Sunday the 26th – in two days I get to leave Rehab. What a long nine months it has been – definitely the hardest thing I have ever gone through and accomplished! Never in my whole life did I think I would end up in a court ordered rehab facility, away from my kids, my husband, my mom, my life. I had really lost my passion to live.

The only thing I ever wanted in life was to be a good mom and I was at the point where I didn't even care about that anymore. Alcohol had consumed my life. I am so grateful today that I was sent here. I am so excited to be moving on to the next journey in my life. I am so happy that I have absolutely *NO* desire to ever drink again — well at least today I don't. *(One day at a time!)*

I have self-worth again. I have energy, enthusiasm, hope and faith again. I feel *AMAZING*! I really want to thank you for all of your encouraging words and all the faith you have in me. I could never have made it through this place without you. I am so blessed to have you as my mom.

I am very sorry for making you worry when I was drinking. I can't even imagine how you must have felt. I know that I would feel so much pain and sorrow if one of my boys were suffering from an addiction. I hope I never have to deal with that, but if I do, I will stand by their sides, giving them words of encouragement and love, just as you have done for me.

Thank you, Mom!
I love you so much!

Now on to the next chapter of my life!

Love, Liz

PREFACE

My youngest daughter, Liz, and I have always been close even though we are separated by many miles, she in Texas and I in California. In 2006 she and her husband decided to move from their home in California and make a new life in Texas. I hated to see them go and for the first time I really understood how saddened my father was when I decided to relocate with my children many years prior from my home in Wisconsin to California.

After Liz moved, we stayed close, talking on the phone almost every day and visiting in person a couple times a year. After the birth of her fourth baby, she went through a difficult postpartum depression and that's when her excessive drinking began. I really didn't know how to help her except to be loving and supportive via long distance. But I realize now that she needed much more help than I was able to give her over the phone.

When I received the call that she had been charged with a second DUI and court ordered to spend up to nine months in a residential drug and alcohol rehab facility located four hours from her home in Texas, I felt devastated for her. I knew she needed help, but this ruling was unexpected and felt overly harsh. In the rehab facility she was not allowed to receive phone calls or have outside contact for the first several months. She was only allowed to get letters. It was very much like a prison.

So, I meditated on what I could do while she was in the facility that would let her know how much she was loved. I got the idea to send her a postcard-sized inspirational/motivational quote every day. I went online and downloaded several hundred graphical quotes from the Internet, resized them to fit 4-up on a piece of cardstock, printed and cut them out. I ended up with over 300 inspirational cards that I kept in a stack by my rocking chair. Every morning I would wake up at 5AM, pick a card and hand write her a personal note on the back. Often I wrote several notes a day. I bought a large box of 4"x 5" envelopes that I pre-addressed and hand-decorated in cheery designs with colorful pens in which to mail the notes. Included in the back of this book is a link to a few samples of my decorated envelopes. I made a point to number each card I sent with a corresponding number on the envelope so Liz could easily see if there were any cards missing. (Somehow I didn't trust that she would receive all my mail, but it turns out that she did!)

My husband suggested that I set up a database with a scan of the front of each card and a field where I could record what I had handwritten on the back. In total I mailed her 255 cards. It is because of my husband's suggestion that I am actually able to write this book and share my process with you.

In order to create this self-help, graphical memoir of Liz's journey to recovery, I redesigned 230 of the inspirational/motivational quotes I sent her with my own collection of commercial-use graphics and fonts. Embedded in each graphic, I have included the name(s) of the fonts I used to create the graphic. Because the original quotes I had printed out often didn't list the author, I diligently searched to see if I could attribute each quote accurately. I was able to find many of the authors, but unfortunately not all. So, those I couldn't find I have simply indicated "author unknown." *(If any readers of this book can supply me with the accurate name(s) of the "unknown authors," I would be most appreciative and will include them in a subsequent printing.)*

My hope is that the quotes and personal messages in this book will serve as a guide in helping the reader understand the importance of self-love, how it is a necessary component of personal empowerment and how you can achieve it in your own life. I also hope that it will inspire those who have a loved one in rehab or prison with a way to help them know that they are loved and not forgotten. Simply being reminded of your love and support can make a huge difference in their rehabilitation, recovery and journey toward self-love and empowerment.

~ Carol Hansen Grey

Inspiration Notes

The Journey Begins

You don't have to see the whole staircase. Just take the

FIRST STEP

Font: Bilbo

~ Dr. Martin Luther King, Jr.

I am so very proud of you for taking your first step toward sobriety.

Fonts: QuartierBook & Quigly

~Author Unknown

What I've come to know is that every challenge in life is an opportunity to learn and grow. I encourage you to embrace this healing opportunity.

God grant me the *Serenity* to accept the things I cannot change... *Courage* to change the things I can & *Wisdom* to know the difference.

Fonts: Euphoria Script & Kingthings Petrock ~ Reinhold Niebuhr

This is the prayer that will get you through this challenging time.

You are stronger
than you know,
You are more capable
than you ever dreamed
and
You are loved more
than you could
possibly imagine.

Font: Oregano

~ A. A. Milne, "Winnie the Pooh"

*Just another reminder of your strength,
your capabilities and just how much
you are loved.*

DON'T LOOK BACK.
You're not going
that way!

Font: Komika Text Bold   ~ Mary Engelbreit

*It's good to remember to let go of the past,
to take advantage of the healing opportunities in
the present moment, and know that
the future holds bright promises.*

Keep your face
always toward the
sunshine
and shadows
will fall
behind you.

Font: Bilbo Regular   ~Walt Whitman

It always helps to find something to be grateful for — even if it's something really small.

The worst mistake is not ~~two~~ to make any.

Font: Mightyheart

~ Author Unknown

If we never make any mistakes — we cease to grow. So my advice is to look for the treasure in each mistake, learn from it, and move on!

Be a

rainbow

in someone

else's cloud.

Font: Merri Gables

~ Maya Angelou

No matter how bad you are feeling —
being a rainbow in someone else's cloud
will lift your spirits as you lift theirs.

FAITH

is taking the first step even when you don't see the whole staircase.

Fonts: Charcuterie Serif & Born Ready Upright

~Martin Luther King, Jr.

Have faith that this healing process will lead you to a future filled with amazing gifts and opportunities.

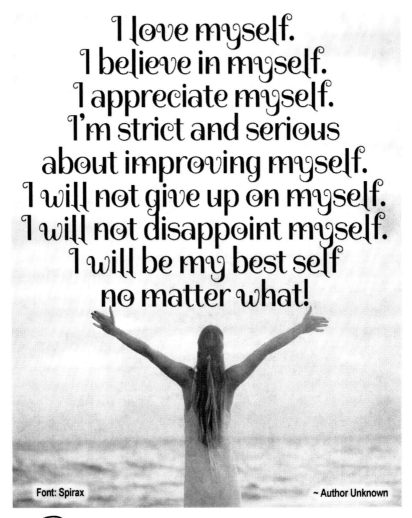

I love myself.
I believe in myself.
I appreciate myself.
I'm strict and serious
about improving myself.
I will not give up on myself.
I will not disappoint myself.
I will be my best self
no matter what!

Font: Spirax   ~ Author Unknown

Read this message to yourself every day, incorporate it into your thought process and watch your life get better and better.

When life is SWEET say Thank You & CELEBRATE

When life is BITTER say Thank You & GROW

Fonts: Born Ready, Peppermint Canes, SBC Curly Outline, LS Leaves   ~ Shauna Niequist

Gratitude is the key to happiness and growth. Even when things are not going the way you'd like them to go, find something in your life to be grateful for and your spirits will be lifted.

We delight in the beauty of the butterfly, but rarely admit the changes it has gone through to achieve that beauty.

Font: Bonheur Royale

— Maya Angelou

The difficulties you are going through right now will all be worth it when you emerge from your dark cocoon as the beautiful being that you truly are!

FOCUS ON WHAT MATTERS

Font: Beloved Sans Bold

~Mom

There are lots of things that can distract us from achieving our goals in life. Take time to decide what's important in your life, focus on that and clear away all the other clutter.

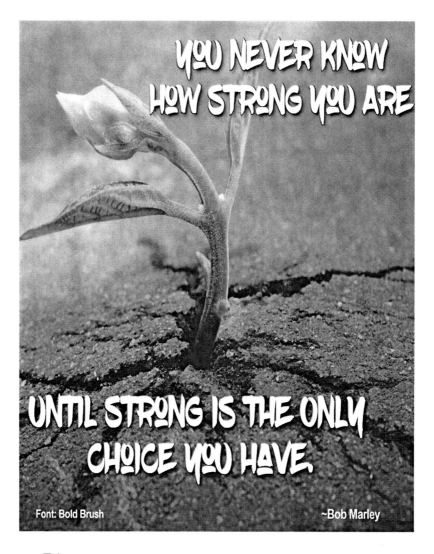

YOU NEVER KNOW HOW STRONG YOU ARE

UNTIL STRONG IS THE ONLY CHOICE YOU HAVE.

Font: Bold Brush

~Bob Marley

Your strength will get you through this challenge and help you accomplish all your goals.

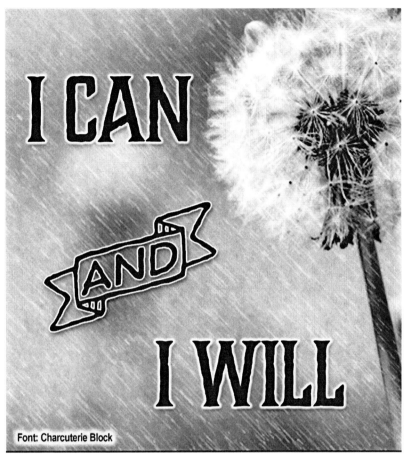

Font: Charcuterie Block

You can and you will survive this
challenging time in your life. You must
trust and never lose faith that everything you
are going through right now will make you a
stronger, more resilient and powerful person.
I have faith in you.
You must have faith in yourself.

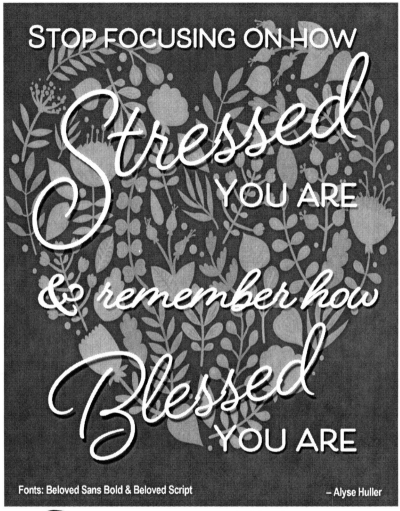

STOP FOCUSING ON HOW

Stressed

YOU ARE

& remember how

Blessed

YOU ARE

Fonts: Beloved Sans Bold & Beloved Script

– Alyse Huller

It is difficult to see how blessed you are when stress obscures your vision. Free yourself by asking that all your negative thoughts be transformed. When the transformation takes place your mind will be filled with positive thoughts.

Font: Aquarelle ~Mom

*A good exercise to do is to close your eyes, put
your hands over your heart and breathe deeply.
Imagine that every breath carries with it
the love that you feel for your family
and the love we feel for you!
Feel yourself filled with love.*

You are worth it all!

Font: Bahia Script

~Mom

Whenever you get discouraged and feel that this healing journey you are on is not worth the effort -- I want you to remember that you are worth it!

Be Yourself!

Everyone else is taken.

Font: Blacksword   ~ Oscar Wilde

You came into this world to be a unique expression of God. There is no other being just like you. You are one of a kind. So, it is important that you express your uniqueness by being yourself.

I love you
to the
moon

& back.

Font: Bilbo Swash Caps

Sam McBratney, author:
"Guess How Much I Love You"

Sending this along... just in case you needed another reminder of how much I love you!

A daughter is a joy forever.

Font: Ambassador Script

~Mom

You have, from the moment you were born,
filled my heart with joy!
I love you so dearly.

These are great reminders of how important it is to live your life to the fullest, no matter what challenges you are facing.

Don't let people discourage you...

Just fluff out your tutu and dance away.

Font: BonheurRoyale

~ Author Unknown

This is such a cute reminder to surround yourself with positive, supportive people and to "dance away" from those who discourage you or bring you down. You don't need their energy in your life.

The only impossible journey is the one you never begin.

Font: Bonheur Royale

~ Anthony Robbins

Whenever you get discouraged remember that you are on a healing journey -- one that is not easy but one that will enable you to be a stronger, happier and healthier person. Be proud of yourself!

It's not what you win...
but how you conquer it.

HEALTH IS INNER PEACE

Fonts: Beloved Sans and Samantha

~ Author Unknown

Someday you will look back at this journey
and be proud of yourself for taking the steps
you needed to take, to create for yourself a
happy and fulfilling life.
I'm so proud of you.

Font: Bonheur Royale   ~Mom

*Each one of us has a light within us-- our job
is to always allow our inner light to shine.
We should never allow anyone or any
circumstance to diminish our light.
Our light is our gift to the world.*

Magic is believing in yourself. If you can do that, you can make anything. happen.

Fonts: Carolyna Woo Curvy & Arial

~ Goethe

I am a true believer in magic and I know because of that belief, I've created for myself a magical life. I know that you can do the same —just believe!

Not all of us can do **GREAT** things, but we can do SMALL things, with great LOVE.

~ Mother Teresa

Fonts: Caprizant, Charcuterie Block, Charcuterie Sans Inline, Heartland

It is always good to remember that even a small act of kindness is better than a grand intention that was never accomplished. Everyday try to do one small act of kindness -- if everyone did this it would change the world.

You know great things are coming when everything seems to be going wrong. Old energy is clearing out for new energy to enter.

Be patient!

Font: Born Ready Slanted

~ Idil Ahmed

This is a great way to think about what you might be perceiving as a negative experience — shifting your perception and looking for the good in every experience is a great way to find happiness in life.

Don't be ashamed of your story!

It will inspire others.

Fonts: Designers Bold & Born Ready Upright   ~ Author Unknown

I envision, in the not too distant future, that your story, when shared with others, will be the spark that will start their healing process.

You get in life what you have the courage to ask for.

Font: Caprizant

~ Oprah Winfrey

Sometimes it is hard to ask for what you want, but the worse that could happen is that the answer might be 'no.' However, in all likelihood the answer will be 'yes.' If you don't ask, you'll never know and you go through life wondering whether or not you should have asked.

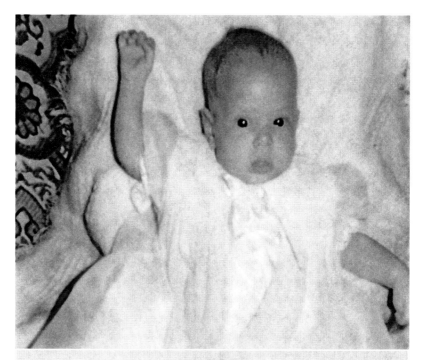

*You are the poem I dreamed of writing,
the masterpiece I longed to paint.
You are the shining star I reached for
in my ever hopeful quest for life fulfilled.
You are my child.
Now with all things, I am blessed.*

Font: BonheurRoyale

~ Oksana Rus

*From the moment I found out I was
pregnant with you, I knew something
magical had happened in my life.
You have always been my magical child.*

Be so
HAPPY
that when others
look at you, they become
HAPPY
too!

Fonts: Komika Text & KBJumpingJellybeans

~ Yogi Bhajan

Happiness is contagious. When you are happy, you energetically send out ripples of happiness that touch and affect others. They, in turn, send out their own ripples and pretty soon everyone has caught the happiness wave!

33

The thing that counts most in the pursuit of happiness…

is choosing the right company!

Font: Bilbo Swash Caps

~Finding Zem

Nothing does more to hurt your morale than being around people who don't love and appreciate you. When you find people like that in your life — let them go with love and seek the companionship of more positive people.

You hold the keys to your own happiness!

Font: Born Ready

~ Sherold Barr

It's always helpful to remember that you DO hold the key to your own happiness. Never surrender that key to someone else expecting them to make you happy. The KEY is yours and yours alone! You must use it to make your own happiness.

When we remember that everyday,
through our thoughts and actions,
we are planting seeds that will take root
and bloom in our future, we can then
understand how important it is
to plant wisely.

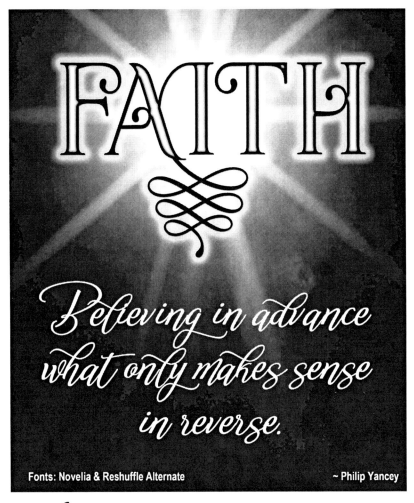

FAITH

Believing in advance what only makes sense in reverse.

Fonts: Novelia & Reshuffle Alternate

~ Philip Yancey

This is a beautiful way of describing "faith." Sometimes it's hard to understand why things happen the way they do until we look back on it. From that future perspective, the gift in each experience can reveal itself, if we are open to finding it.

LIFE is an ever shifting kaleidoscope, a slight change and all patterns alter.

Fonts: Sheila & Spirax

~ Sharon Salzberg

Thinking of life as an ever shifting kaleidoscope may help you think differently about how you can change undesirable patterns in your life. I encourage you to embrace this time of change and envision how beautiful your life can be.

Fonts: LOT Threads Karen & Mandevilla Bold   ~ Kim Beaupre

I love this simple, yet powerful message.
May your life be filled with every good thing
you've ever hoped for and may you be filled
with love and joy that comes back to you as
you radiate it out!

Fonts: Euphoria Script & Mighty Heart   ~Deanna Heiliger

I know you love to exercise, so I encourage you to add this to your daily exercise routine. As you work out, mentally list everything you can think of that brings you joy. Using your body and mind in this way will fill you with joy as you radiate it out!

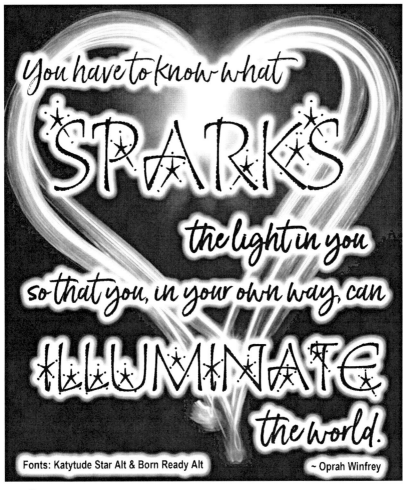

Fonts: Katytude Star Alt & Born Ready Alt

~ Oprah Winfrey

Each of us has a light within us but until we understand and find what sparks that light, it can remain hidden. The spark is ignited by knowing and doing what brings you joy. Once you are on your joy-filled path, your inner light will illuminate the world.

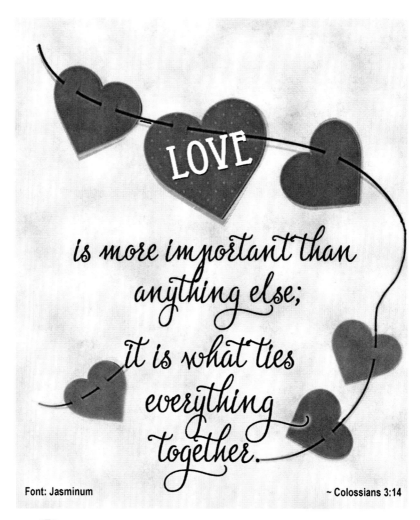

LOVE is more important than anything else; It is what ties everything together.

Font: Jasminum

~ Colossians 3:14

I truly believe that each of us was born into this world to learn this lesson of love -- love of ourselves, love of others, love of our beautiful planet. Without love, nothing makes sense -- with love everything falls into place.

I have chosen to be

HAPPY

because it's good
for my health.

Fonts: Bilbo & ZnikomitNo24

~ Voltaire

Happiness is a choice, so I encourage you to choose to be happy. It may seem difficult at first but the more you focus on and work towards what makes you happy, the easier it becomes to be happy. Studies have shown that happy people are healthier people. Here's to your health and happiness.

Do what makes
you happy,
be with who makes
you smile,
laugh as much as
you breathe,
and love as long
as you live.

Font: Bilbo Swash Caps

~ Rachel Ann Nunes

I feel this message is the secret to living an amazing life. "Do what makes you happy, be with who makes you smile, laugh as much as you breathe, and love as long as you live." Sending you lots of happy, loving thoughts today.

Start each day
with a grateful
heart!

Font: Broadway Alt4 Regular   ~ Author Unknown

A great habit to cultivate when you wake up
each morning is to take a minute or so to
make a mental list of everything in your life
that you're grateful for -- your health, your
family, your friends, etc. Give it a try!

The design of this message is quite clever —
"DON'T QUIT" turning into "DO IT"
"DON'T QUIT" is a passive thought.
"DO IT" is an action!
Both are required for change to take place.

46

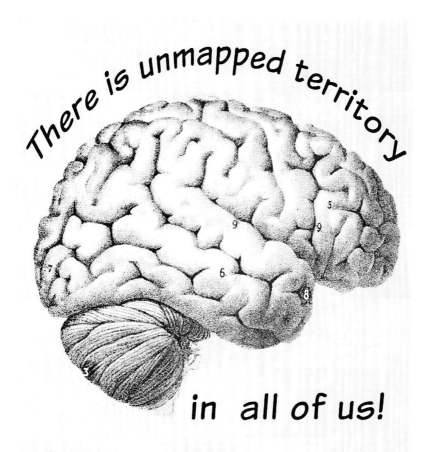

There is unmapped territory

in all of us!

Font: Komika Text   ~ Walt Disney

*Use this opportunity to chart and explore
new ways of thinking and being that will
best serve you on your life path.
Be open to new insights your exploration
will reveal and trust that
it's all part of your growth process.*

POSITIVE THOUGHTS
generate

POSITIVE FEELINGS
& attract

POSITIVE LIFE
experiences.

Fonts: Uptight Hollow & Lovers Quarrel   ~Mae West

This is a theme that I will be sending you frequently -- the importance of keeping your thoughts positive. Not only does it make you feel better, it helps those around you feel better, too!

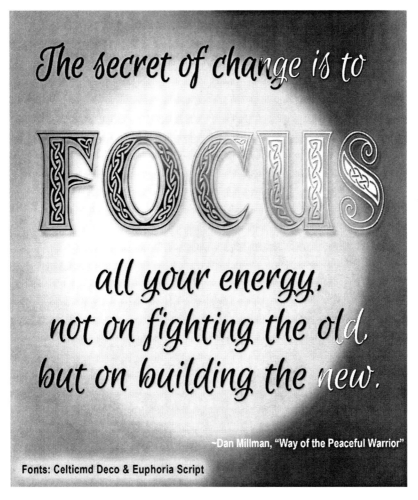

The secret of change is to **FOCUS** all your energy, not on fighting the old, but on building the new.

~Dan Millman, "Way of the Peaceful Warrior"

Fonts: Celticmd Deco & Euphoria Script

This is a good way to think about change. Don't expend your energy fighting what you want to change in your life. Instead focus your energy on building a new way of being — a way that brings you happiness, joy and inner peace.

I CHOOSE...

to live by choice, not by chance;
to make changes, not excuses;
to be motivated, not manipulated;
to be useful, not used;
to excel, not compete.
I CHOOSE SELF-ESTEEM,
not self pity.
I CHOOSE TO LISTEN
to my inner voice,
not the random opinions of others.

Fonts: QuartierBook & QuotaLight

~Miranda Marrott

In life we have lots of choices on how we live our time on this planet. Here are some of the important choices we can make that will serve us and empower us to live a meaningful life. We are always at choice in everything we do.

Fonts: SBC Curly Outline and Christina   ~ Colonel John McCrae

*This light and playful design carries a
powerful message. What it says to me
is that it's important to work each day
to achieve our goals with joy!*

I know for sure that what we dwell on is who we become.

Font: BonheurRoyale

~Oprah Winfrey

It is so important to pay attention to our thoughts, because thought is the creative force in our lives. Without thought there is NO creativity. Therefore, dwell on the life you wish to create for yourself instead of dwelling on past mistakes and you will achieve your goals.

Fonts: Kidlit Alphabet3, Kidlit Regular, LOT Threads Karen, HeartlandRegular

This message is simply a reminder to you of how much I love you. You have and always will hold a special place in my heart. Sending you lots of love today, and always.

God's plan for your life is BIGGER than everything that is coming against it.

Fonts: Carolyna Woo & Zenfyrkalt

~Kenneth Copeland

Sometimes we face obstacles in our life that seem to be too big to overcome. That's when it is good to remember that God DOES have a plan for each of us — we are not here by accident!

Trust that everything you are experiencing will somehow fit into the bigger picture of God's plan.

Font: Great Vibes   ~Doreen Virtue

Your self-love and approval is the most important gift you can give yourself. Without it you will be unable to accept the love and approval of others in your life. Love begins with you!

Stay Patient & trust your journey.

Font: Novelia

~ Author Unknown

Often we don't know or understand why we are facing certain challenges. I feel, at those times, that it is important to be patient and to trust that we are being guided to grow and evolve into a higher, better version of ourselves. Trust your journey.

ALWAYS

bring your own sunshine!

Font: Harrington   ~Anthony D'Angelo

I've learned that it's best not to rely on others to bring "light" into your life. Tap into the abundant light you have within you and let it shine for all to see. In that way you bring your own sunshine wherever you go!

There are far better things ahead

than any we leave behind.

Font: Bilbo Swash Caps   ~ C. S. Lewis

It's important to trust while you are on
this healing journey that a better life lies
ahead — one where you are healthy
and strong and living a life
that brings you joy!

PeFECTiON

is an idea that exists only in the mind, not in reality!

Font: Al DancingEgypt

~ Author Unknown

This is a great reminder: "Perfection is an idea that exists only in the mind, not in reality." I have known people who are miserable because their life isn't their idea of "perfect." If you want to be happy, give up the goal of "perfection."

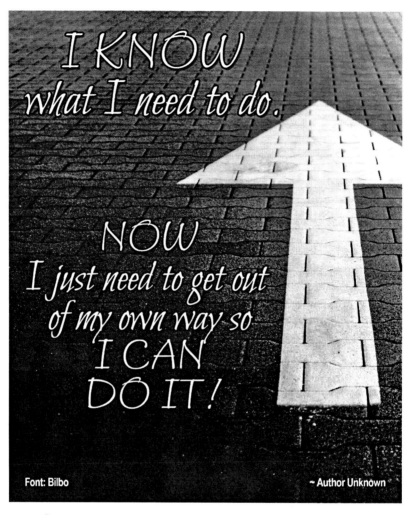

Sometimes all we need to accomplish a goal is a simple reminder that you know what to do and how to do it. You simply need to drop your resistance and move forward!

No one ever injured
their eyesight
by looking on the

BRIGHT

side of things!

Fonts: Brightlight & Burst ~ Author Unknown

Even when your situation appears gloomy, it's a worthwhile exercise to step into the sunlight by transforming your gloomy thoughts to make way for positive, sunny thoughts to fill your mind. Staying in the gloom will just make things seem worse. Please force yourself to step out of the gloom into the light.

It is important that you put your
well-being and recovery as your top priority right
now so that the journey you are on right now will
not have been in vain. I have faith in you and
know you are strong enough to get through this.

Dear Past...
Thank you for your lessons.

Dear Future...
I'm ready.

Dear God...
Thank you for another chance.

Fonts: Relish & BahiaScript

~ Author Unknown

When we can embrace our past with gratitude for the lessons it has taught us, we can then look forward to a brighter future. Gratitude is the key!

I want to be clear & definite
about the important things in life.

I want to have a strong sense
of who I am.

I want to cherish the past
but also realize that things
do not stay the same.

And God will continue to bless me
as life changes.

Font: Bilbo   ~Lorna Steeb

Be clear and definite about what is important in your life, have a strong sense of who you are, and cherish the past for its lessons as you move forward into a fuller, happier life. Know that you are loved and blessed.

It is worthwhile to acknowledge what you're going
through right now — "It is what it is."
Your job is to find the gift in each experience
so you can move on as you heal.
Know that you are loved and blessed.

Negative people need
drama like it was oxygen.

Stay positive & take
their breath away!

Fonts: Charcuterie Engraved. Glitter, BreezeStarboards

– Tony Gaskins

I know it is sometimes difficult to stay positive
especially if you are surrounded by negative
people who are addicted to **DRAMA**.
Just remember that you don't have to
accept a role in their "movie."
The choice between negative and positive is yours.

66

A little **spark** of kindness can put a colossal **BURST OF SUNSHINE** into someone's day.

Fonts: Bembo, Sabrina Star, Firebug, Gonzo

– Jen@AimHappy.com

I try to do at least one anonymous good deed every day — it might be as simple as slowing down to allow someone to pull into traffic, or picking up something someone has dropped, or smiling and wishing someone a good day. Practicing kindness, I feel, is one way each of us can contribute to making the world a better place for us all.

Find joy in the ordinary

Font: Saturday Script

~Mom

When you feel you are in a joyless place, that's when it's most important to find joy in the ordinary — * a roof over your head (even though it may not be the roof you'd prefer to be under — it's still protecting you), * shoes on your feet, * a bed to sleep on, * food to eat, etc.

The STRUGGLE

you are in today
is developing the

STRENGTH

you will need for
tomorrow.

Fonts: Born Ready Upright, Brad, Great Lakes Shadow   ~ Robert Tew

Sending you lots of blessings today.
I know this journey has not been an easy one.
So this note is just a reminder that better
days are ahead and you are loved
more than words can say.

69

LIFE IS THE ART OF DRAWING WITHOUT AN ERASER.

Font: Avaline Script

~John W. Gardner

I love this way of looking at life.
We can't erase our past mistakes -- what is
important is that we learn from them and then
move forward envisioning and creating the life
we truly desire. Often the biggest "mistakes"
we make in our lives become our greatest
learning experiences.

The cells in your body react to everything that your mind says.

Negativity brings down your immune system.

Font: Blacksword   ~ Deepak Chopra

This message explains why it's so important for your health and well-being to fill your mind with positive thoughts. When negative thoughts creep in, use the Free Yourself from Fear process* to transform the thought. I encourage you to be diligent and reap the rewards of a positive mind-set.

*See Free Yourself from Fear at https://openheartpress.com/pages/fyf-online

FAILURE

is nothing more than a chance to revise your strategy.

Fonts: Blowbrush, Bembo

~Sissy Gavrilaki

I heard a successful business woman being interviewed recently. She was asked to what she could attribute her success. She said it was a family custom that her father had started. At dinner each night she, with her parents and siblings, would have to report what their greatest failure was that day and what they learned from it. No one was ever put down for a failure, but were celebrated for having learned from it. She therefore never thought of failure as a bad thing, but rather as a series of stepping stones to great accomplishments.

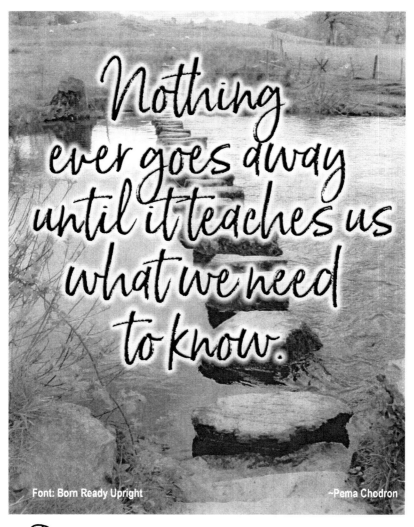

Nothing ever goes away until it teaches us what we need to know.

Font: Born Ready Upright

~Pema Chodron

I truly believe that each of us are on this planet for a reason and that we are continuously being given lessons that enable us to grow to our full potential. It's our job to learn each lesson, grow from it, then move to the next lesson.

It's a Journey... No one is ahead of you or behind you.
You are not more "advanced" or less enlightened.
You are exactly where you need to be.
It's not a Contest... It's LIFE!
We are ALL teachers
and we are ALL
students.

Photo by Vikramjit Kakati

~ Author Unknown

Font: BodegaSans-Medium

It's always good to be reminded that life is a journey and not a contest. Your only job is to learn and apply your lessons and keep moving forward by helping others along the way.

Some see
a weed.

Some see
a wish.

Font: Brightlight

~ Author Unknown

Enjoying life and making the most of it really boils down to keeping a positive attitude. When life throws you a curve-ball, look at it as an opportunity to see things with a new perspective as you continue to learn and grow.

I choose to make the rest of my life

the BEST of my LIFE!

Font: Harrington ~ Louise Hay

We are always "at choice." We can choose to focus
on past mistakes and bemoan our current situation ...
or we can choose to have a positive mind-set,
looking at each life event as a lesson to
help us grow and lead a fulfilling life.

Font: Broadway Regular ~Katrina Mayer

I feel that the best way to attain inner and outer peace is for each of us to take responsibility to plant seeds of love everywhere we go. A seed may be as small as a smile to a stranger, or as large as volunteering your time to help someone in need. Planting seeds of love changes our world.

May the
blessings
of the light
be on you--
light within and
light without!

Font: Honey Script SemiBold

~ Old Irish Blessing

*Sending you lots of love and blessings today
that you may be surrounded with and filled
with light as you continue your
journey toward sobriety.*

Font: Dectari Script   ~ Author Unknown

Everyone needs some type of emotional support from time to time. A good deed you could perform everyday would be to give emotional support when you see that someone is having a bad day. In other word's you could "be someone's umbrella" by sheltering them from the rain while showering them with words of encouragement. Every good deed you perform, even though it might seem small, is never wasted.

Old ways won't *open* new doors.

Fonts: Charcuterie Serif & Saturday Script Oblique   ~ Author Unknown

It's good to remember that if we want to create new possibilities for positive change in our lives, we need to let go of old habits and focus on creating new ways that will open doors to a more fulfilling life.

I am in competition with no one.
I have no desire to play the game of being better than anyone.
I am simply trying to be better than the person I was yesterday.

Font: Designers Bold

~ Selena Gomez

We are indoctrinated into the world of competition at a very early age. It is important that we recognize how damaging it is to constantly compare ourselves to others. The only important comparison to consider is whether or not I am becoming a new and improved version of myself.

You cannot start the next chapter of your life if you keep re-reading the last one.

Font: Bilbo Swash Caps

~ Michael McMillan

It is important to recognize that you are in the process of starting the next chapter of your life. You are the author of your life story and it is up to you to determine how the next chapter will unfold. Write a script filled with happiness and love.

You are:
GOOD enough,
SMART enough,
BEAUTIFUL enough &
STRONG enough.
Believe it and never let
insecurity run your life.

Font: Relish   ~ Author Unknown

It is so important that you believe in yourself and
what you are capable of accomplishing. Believe that
you are strong enough, good enough, smart enough
and beautiful enough to accomplish every goal you
truly desire and are willing to work toward.
Once you embed those beliefs into your consciousness,
you will achieve everything your heart desires.

Endurance

is the price

tag of

Achievement.

Font: Silver Script Flourishes

~ Austin Chakaodza

You are in a situation now that is definitely testing your endurance and in the process you are becoming a stronger, wiser woman. You are developing strength and stamina to face and conquer your life's challenges with grace and fortitude. I am so very proud of you!

Sometimes when we find ourselves in an environment where we are continually being criticized — that is the time when it is most important to remember that we are each a child of God and deserving of love. Love yourself — it is the most important thing you can do to honor the gift God has given you . . . Life!

I have complete faith in your ability to take what you need to learn from this experience and come out at the end of this challenging time a stronger and more powerful woman. You Got This!

**DON'T
QUIT YOUR
DAY DREAM!**

Font: Bembo Bold Italic   ~ Mom

I can imagine that in your situation you probably don't have much time, energy or inclination to daydream about your future. But I encourage you to do so. Think about what you want to do with your life after rehab and then allow yourself to daydream about it and . . . you **WILL** *attract it.*

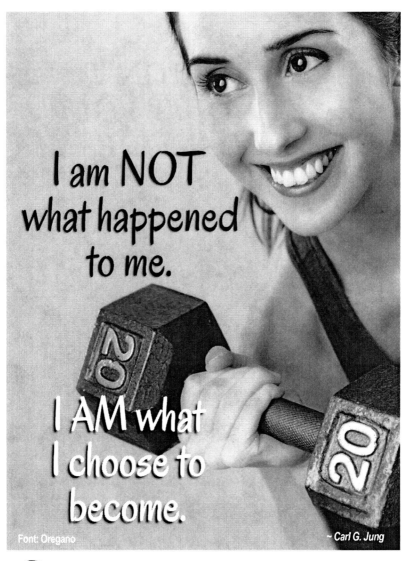

I am NOT what happened to me.

I AM what I choose to become.

Font: Oregano

~ Carl G. Jung

I've learned that it is important to never define myself by my past failures or successes. What is important is to live in the present moment while envisioning the future you desire (and choose) to attract.

I'VE NEVER MET A STRONG PERSON WITH AN EASY PAST!

Font: Komika Parch

~ Nicky Gumbel

It's good to remember that everything you've been through and are currently experiencing will make you a stronger person if that is what you desire. Never let your past define you. Grow from each experience. Be the strong, beautiful woman you truly are!

BLOOM

where you are planted.

Fonts: Flores & Merri Gables

~ Jane Hoff

"Bloom where you are planted" is a good philosophy to live by. We can't always choose where we'd like to be in life, but we **can** choose our attitude and how we react to our current situation. I encourage you to choose to bloom!

How you **VIBRATE** is what the *Universe echoes back to you in every moment.*

Fonts: Honey Script & Bungnipper ~Panache

Your thoughts create your personal vibration and your vibration ripples outward attracting to you the energy (or vibration) of those thoughts. By focusing on positive thoughts, you can change your vibration to attract your deepest dreams and desires.

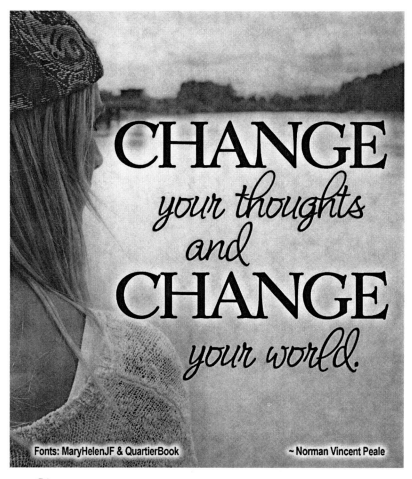

CHANGE *your thoughts* *and* CHANGE *your world.*

Fonts: MaryHelenJF & QuartierBook   ~ Norman Vincent Peale

You know how important it is to your well-being and your happiness to pay attention to your thoughts. When negative or limiting thoughts intrude into your consciousness, squash them immediately by demanding from your Higher Power that they be transformed. Then focus on "good feeling" thoughts to keep your vibration high.

Positive change happens when you

CHANGE YOUR THOUGHTS

CHANGE YOUR FEELINGS

CHANGE YOUR ACTIONS

Fonts: Bellagio and Majestic Bold ~ Lynda Field

You are the only one who can create how you feel about each and every experience. I encourage you to tell yourself a "good feeling" story about your experiences in rehab and watch yourself feel better physically, mentally and emotionally.

CREATE THE HIGHEST, GRANDEST VISION POSSIBLE FOR YOUR LIFE, BECAUSE YOU BECOME WHAT YOU BELIEVE.

Font: Beloved Sans

~ Oprah Winfrey

It is within your power to create the life of your dreams. The only necessary component is your willingness to change your thoughts.
Use your imagination to visualize the highest, grandest vision of yourself, ask your Higher Self to transform any thoughts that are not in alignment with that vision and to enhance every good, positive thought.

If you realized how powerful your thoughts were you would never think a negative thought again.

Font: Cherryla

~Peace Pilgrim

We have talked many times about the power of our thoughts. This inspiration is a good reminder.
You attract what you think about.
Think good thoughts... even when you would rather bitch and moan.
You'll be happier... and that's the goal.

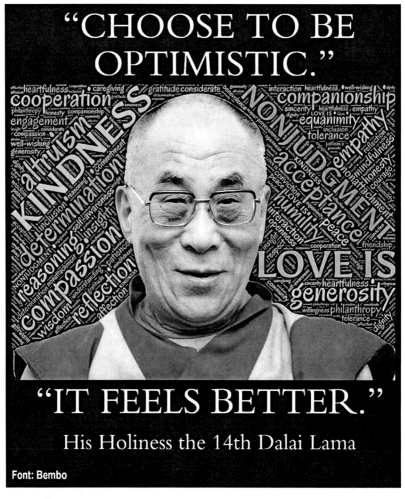

"CHOOSE TO BE OPTIMISTIC."

"IT FEELS BETTER."

His Holiness the 14th Dalai Lama

Font: Bembo

Being optimistic is a choice we can each make, despite whatever situation we find ourselves going through. Wallowing in pessimism will only make the situation feel worse than it needs to feel. Take the Dalai Lama's advice and choose optimism . . . just because it feels better!

The ultimate reason for meditating is to transform ourselves in order to be better able to transform the world.

Font: Good Vibrations

~Matthieu Ricard

I honestly believe that bringing yourself into a state of inner peace through meditation is truly a way of helping, not only yourself, but also helping to create peace in the world.

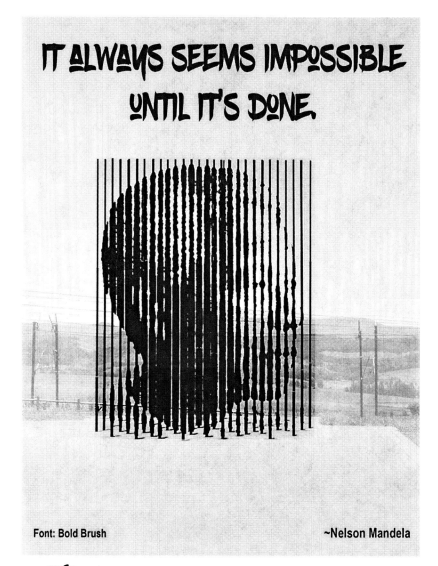

IT ALWAYS SEEMS IMPOSSIBLE UNTIL IT'S DONE.

Font: Bold Brush   ~Nelson Mandela

The hardest part about achieving a goal is first to believe it can be done. Once you've got that belief in place, then your job is to pursue it with all your heart and let nothing stand in your way.

Don't let comparison steal your joy!

Fonts: Mandevilla Bold & Qwigley

~ Author Unknown

Everyone is unique in their own way, so to compare your unique abilities and gifts to someone else's is truly a waste of time and energy. It is a much wiser and more fulfilling path to continue to hone your own uniqueness.

Fonts: QuartierBook, Jacoba

~Mom

I have discovered that I can use 'joy' as my gauge
to determine the direction in my life. If it is not
bringing me joy, I choose a different path.
I encourage you to give it a try!
It is a joyous way to live a happy life.

You were given this
LIFE
because you are
STRONG
enough to live it!

Font: Harrington — Ain Eineziz

I truly believe with all my heart that you are strong enough to overcome any obstacle in your path. Let every obstacle be a lesson that serves to make you a stronger, wiser woman.

DO the right thing... even when no one is looking!

Font: Euphoria Script

~ C.S. Lewis

Doing the right thing even when no one is looking is good for your soul because someone is always looking...
your "Higher Self", who knows all and sees all and showers you with blessings every time you do good.!

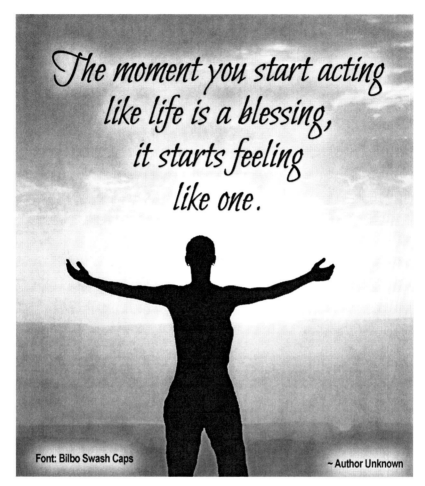

The moment you start acting like life is a blessing, it starts feeling like one.

Font: Bilbo Swash Caps

~ Author Unknown

Many people spend a lot of time complaining about things that have happened in their lives and living with regrets. What they fail to understand is that the more they complain, the more they attract that which they are complaining about. Shifting their thoughts to seeing their life as a blessing will actually create a blessed reality.

Font: Born Ready

~ Michael Eisen

We all need some 'alone time' in our lives to recharge and to get in touch with what's important to us -- to really get to know who we are and what we want to achieve in life. You might find that your 'alone time' becomes the most important part of your

Imagination is everything. It is the preview of life's coming attractions.

Font: Broadway Alt4

~Albert Einstein

I have shared with you many of my manifestation stories. What they all have in common is that I've used my imagination to intensely focus on one thing at a time, envisioning it coming true. So while you are in rehab I hope you will imagine each aspect of the life you want to create for yourself. Focus on just one thing at a time and envision it coming true. It works!

Suddenly
all my ancestors are behind me.

"Be still," they say.
"Watch and listen.
You are the result of
the love of thousands!"

Font: Avalanche Script TT   ~ Linda Hogan

I think it is good every once in a while
to reflect in gratitude on our ancestors
and the love that enabled us
to be here now —
in this body,
in this family,
in this time.

EVERYTHiNG Happens for a reason.

Font: BabOonjaZzbaSsoOn & Desigers Bold

~ Marilyn Monroe

It's true — everything does happen for a reason.
Our job is to discover the reason and grow
from the experience. In that way we can view
every experience as a blessing.

Because
there is only
one
of you in all of
time & space,
your
expression
is unique.

Fonts: Sheila & Taxidermist II ~ Martha Graham

It's interesting how many people measure their worth
by comparing themselves to others instead of
celebrating their uniqueness.
It's good to remember that you are

ONE OF A KIND

and have unique gifts to share with the world.

108

Be Yourself
Accept Yourself
Value Yourself
Forgive Yourself
Bless Yourself
Express Yourself
Trust Yourself
Love Yourself
Empower Yourself

Font: Kidlit Alphabet1

~Mom

Here are nine of my
Personal Empowerment Cards*
all rolled into one graphic.
If one could master just the nine listed here...
most of their "perceived" limitations
would immediately dissolve.

*See <openheartpress.com/products/personal-empowerment-deck>

The smallest act of kindness is worth more than the GRANDEST intention.

Fonts: Love Light & Charcuterie Serif

~Oscar Wilde

A great habit to cultivate is to commit to doing at least one "good deed" or act of kindness everyday, without any expectation of a thank you or acknowledgment. Doing this creates a positive energy within yourself that radiates out into the world, serving you as the giver as well as the receiver.

By changing nothing, nothing changes.

Font: Bembo

~ Tony Robbins

Sometimes we may feel hopeless about a situation we find ourselves experiencing. At those times it's important to realize the Universe is sending us a message. So instead of feeling hopeless, gather your courage and be willing to take the steps necessary to create the changes you need to make to step out of 'hopeless' into empowerment.

When you can
tell your story
and it doesn't
make you cry,
you know you
have healed.

Font: Angelique   ~Inspiration Quotes Gazette

Sharing our stories helps us heal.
I hope you find the opportunity to tell your story
enough times that you can heal all the hurt
you have buried deep inside.
Sending you lots of love today and always,

Font: Golly Gosh   ~C.S. Lewis

This is a good reminder that we shouldn't limit our goals and dreams because of our age. As long as we are blessed to be alive, we can continue to pursue the dreams that are important to us!

LIFE is like
a road trip...
enjoy each day
& don't carry
too much
baggage!

NEXT
50 YEARS

Font: Kaushan Script

~ Author Unknown

If you think of life as a road trip and you make a commitment to enjoy the journey, you will find the time goes faster. The detour you are on right now is filled with potholes and bumps in the road, but if you can think of it as simply a relatively short detour in your life and choose to keep a positive attitude, you'll be better able to endure the bumps.

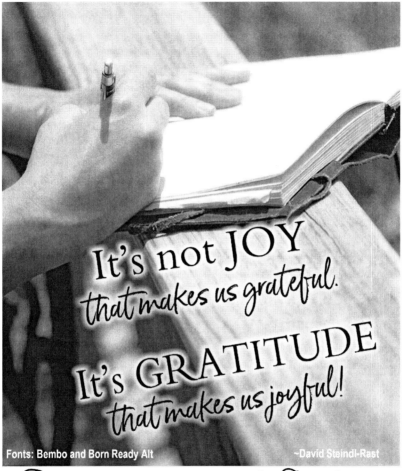

It's not JOY
that makes us grateful.

It's GRATITUDE
that makes us joyful!

Fonts: Bembo and Born Ready Alt   ~David Steindl-Rast

I encourage you to practice gratitude. A simple way to do that is by using a Gratitude Journal. Even if you are unhappy with your life right now, there is always some small thing that you can be grateful for. Try to write a gratitude everyday, even if it's just one or two words. You don't have to fill up the page, but it would be helpful if you dated each entry so when you look back you will be able to see your progress.

Sometimes
the dreams
that come
true
are the dreams
you never even
knew you had.

Font: Laureen

~ Alice Sebold

Life is always full of surprises and some of them
feel horrible when they happen. But I can
assure you there is a gift in every experience.
Just be open to discovering the gift
and it will make the experience
more bearable (and later on — understandable).

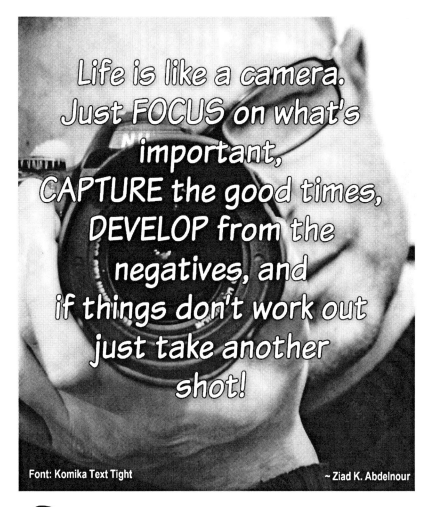

I absolutely love this message — to think of life like a camera by focusing on what's important, capturing the good times, developing (i.e., learning from) the negatives, and if things don't work out— take another shot (i.e., take a new approach). Hope you get as much out of this message as I did.

Font: Kayleigh   ~ Dr. George Simon

Every morning I end my meditation by telling myself what I'm grateful for. It's a great way to start each day. I hope you will use your gratitude journal to write something in it each day that you're grateful for (and even express it outloud to yourself). It's a wonderful way to set the tone for your day.

HAPPINESS
doesn't come from
BEING
in love.
It comes from
BECOMING
love!

Fonts: Bembo & Black Jack

~ Bailey Brooks

When we are actually able to understand the importance of loving ourselves, just the way we are, that is the first step to knowing that we are love. It is not something we do, it is who we are. Everything we experience that is not love is an opportunity for us to realign with the truth of who we are — to realign with love.

I guess if you don't jump, you'll never know if you can fly.

Font: Bodoni 72

~ Miranda Lambert

This is an important lesson for us all to learn — if you don't pursue your dreams, you'll never know if you can achieve them. Let go of your past mistakes, let go of your guilt, let go of your fears and leap into a new way that is being offered to you of navigating your life.

Whatever you are **BE** a good one!

Fonts: 2Peas Goofball & Buddytalk

~ Abraham Lincoln

We may not always like where we find ourselves at certain points in our life. What's important is that we honor and love ourselves enough to make the best of every situation and to never lose faith that every situation is an opportunity for us to grow.

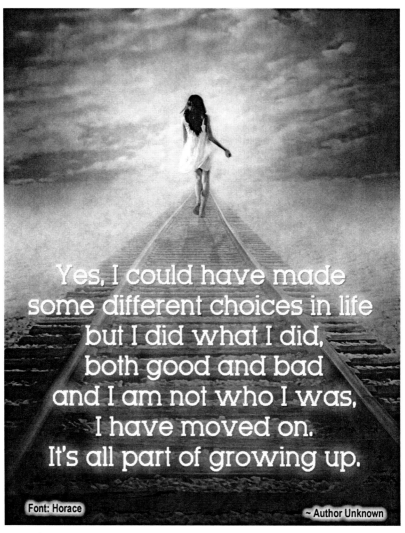

Yes, I could have made
some different choices in life
but I did what I did,
both good and bad
and I am not who I was,
I have moved on.
It's all part of growing up.

Font: Horace

~ Author Unknown

Wallowing in guilt over choices we have made
in life is a useless exercise.
The important thing is to learn
from each experience and to move on
as a strong, wiser person.

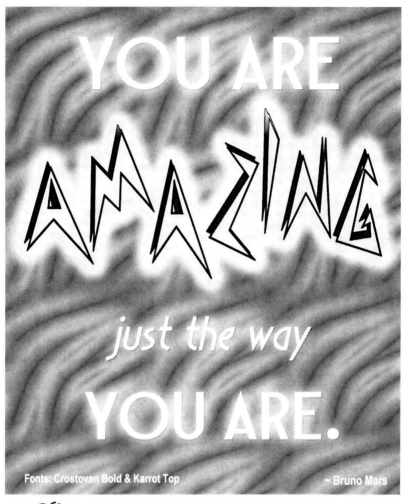

This is a reminder that you are amazing just the way you are -- an amazing woman, daughter, wife, mother and friend. Never give your power away -- cultivate it and let this experience make you stronger, wiser and more empowered than you ever thought possible.

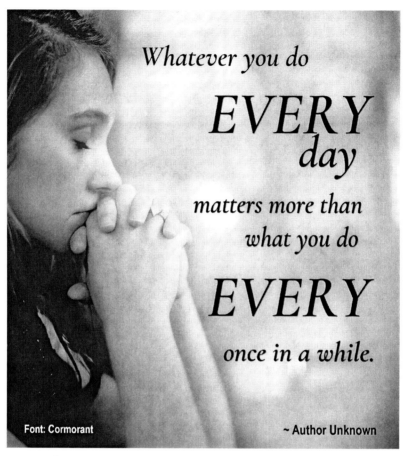

Whatever you do

EVERY
day

matters more than
what you do

EVERY

once in a while.

Font: Cormorant

~ Author Unknown

This message stresses how important it is to your personal growth to make a daily commitment to taking actions that will lead you toward achieving your goals. The actions don't have to be big -- you simply have to be consistent in your choices -- everyday.
You can do this!

Blessed are the *flexible* for they will not be *bent* out of shape.

~ Robert Ludhum

Fonts: Eiffel Falls and Rainy Day Line

This saying, I believe, carries a profound message. I hope you will take it to heart and recognize its wisdom. You want to learn to be a "rubber-band" person — to be resilient. I believe in you and know you have it in you to overcome any setback.

Font: Lovers Quarrel & Lefina
~ Joseph Campbell

One of my favorite bumper stickers is
"Don't follow me... I'm following my Bliss".
I actually think that following your bliss is a
great way to live your life. When you
consciously gravitate toward what makes you
happy, your happiness creates a
ripple effect in the world.

126

Who cares what they think!

Font: Martila ~ Nolan Gould

Never let other people's judgments
stop you from becoming
the fullest and greatest expression of the
unique person that you are!

Love
yourself
first and
everything
else will
fall into
place.

~ Lucille Ball

(It's probaby no coincidence
that her TV show was called
"I Love Lucy")

Font: Annamelia

The most valuable lesson I've learned in this
lifetime, is the importance of loving myself.
If you don't love yourself first, you can't possibly love
others because it would be like trying to give someone
water from empty well. The more you love yourself,
the more love you can give.

Live your life
from your

HEART
and your story
will touch
and heal
people's
SOULS.

Fonts: Allspice Alternates & Madame Roi

~ Melody Beattie

*The healing process you are going through right now
will not only serve to help you become a more
empowered woman, it will also help others with
whom you are guided to share your story.
You will know in your heart who
needs to hear your story.*

The happiest
people don't
HAVE THE BEST
of everything,
they just
MAKE THE BEST
of everything.

Fonts: Lillipip and Lolliplop   ~ Sam Cawthorn

If you can remember to always look for the gift in every experience no matter how difficult it may seem at the time, you will discover the secret to living a happy life..

We are not given
a good life or
a bad life.
We are given a life.
It's up to you
to make it
good or bad.

Font: Kingthings Petrock Light

~ Ward Foley

*The power is within each one of us
to choose the life we wish to live.
It is simply our negative or limiting thoughts
that keep us from achieving our ideal life.
Be willing to identify those thoughts, ask the
Holy Spirit to transform them and you will
open the door to the life you have always
dreamed of living.*

Brain Lateralization

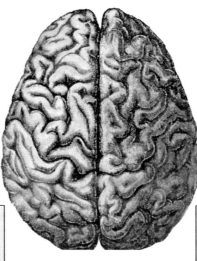

Left

- Analytical thought
- Detail Oriented Perception
- Ordered Sequencing
- Rational Thought
- Verbal
- Cautious
- Planning
- Math/Science
- Logic
- Right Field Vision
- Right Side Motor Skills

Right

- Intuitive Thought,
- Holistic perception
- Random Sequencing
- Emotional Thought
- Non-verbal
- Adventurous
- Impulse
- Creative Writing/Art
- Imagination
- Left Field Vision
- Left Side Motor Skills

It's important that we do exercises to balance the right and left hemispheres of our brains. My computer work keeps my left brain active, while my art work keeps my right brain engaged. Most people tend to favor one side of the brain over the other — but I've always been pretty balanced. Anyway, I thought you might find this graphic informative as it explains the various functions of the left and right brain.

Dear Past...
Thank you for
your lessons.

Dear Future...
I'm ready.

Dear God...
Thank you for
another chance.

Fonts: Just Hello & Dagobert

~ Author Unknown

I am so very grateful that you are getting the help
you need. Each time we get the rare chance to talk
by phone you sound more and more empowered.
I am so very proud of you.

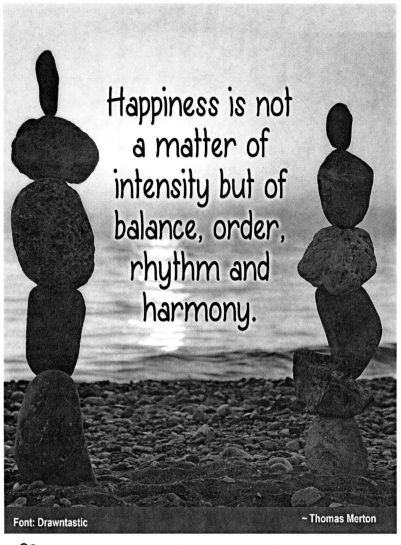

Happiness is not
a matter of
intensity but of
balance, order,
rhythm and
harmony.

Font: Drawntastic

~ Thomas Merton

Everyone experiences happiness in their own unique way. My hope is that you will find the balance, rhythm and harmony in your life that will bring you true happiness.

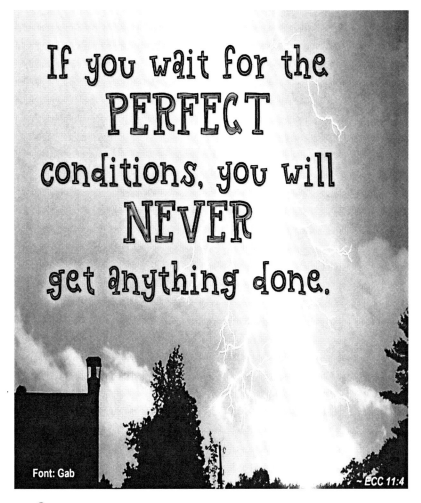

Sometimes the perfect conditions show up at the perfect time for us to take action, but I've found that if I want to accomplish something, the perfect conditions show up **after** I have taken the first step in the direction of my goal. We each personally create the perfect conditions by setting our intention and then taking the necessary action.

Font: Greatest Show

Adapted from Flamingo Print
Artwork by Valerie McKeehan

No matter what situation you find yourself in, don't let it beat you down... stand tall and let your inner strength carry you through. You can do this!

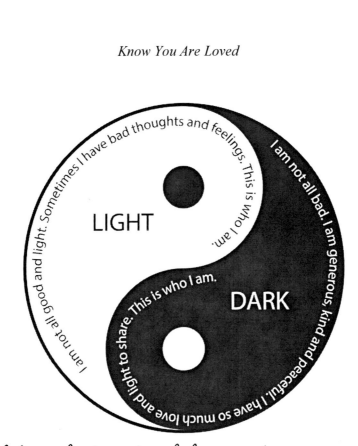

Text in the circle:

LIGHT

DARK

Sometimes I have bad thoughts and feelings. This is who I am. I am not all good and light.

I am not all bad. I am generous, kind and peaceful. I have so much love and light to share. This is who I am.

Life is about creating balance, not suppressing your good, and not suppressing your bad, for one cannot exist without the other. Embrace them equally.

Font: Angelique

~ Author Unknown
Artwork: Carol Hansen Grey

It is helpful to remember that to lead a successful, happy life we must find balance. That doesn't come from denying parts of ourselves, but by acknowledging all aspects of ourselves and balancing the good with the bad.

Breathe in inspiration and trust yourself. The answer is: "Yes, you can!"

Font: Blacksword

~ Author Unknown

Never lose faith in your ability to get through any situation you encounter in your life. If you approach the situation with the right attitude, it will make you stronger. Yes! You can!

No one can do it for you.
Choose to use this time to
develop your wings!

Font: Alana Pro

~ Mom

The situation you are in right now is like a cocoon...
a place where you are developing your wings.
It can feel unpleasant and confining, but it is good to
remember that it is helping to make you stronger
so that when you emerge, you can truly be
empowered to use your wings and fly!

Forgive others,
not because they
deserve forgiveness,
but because you
deserve peace.

Font: Alana PRO

~ Jonathan Lockwood Huie

This graphic points out an important aspect of
forgiveness that is often overlooked...
it brings YOU inner peace.

SO, BE SELFISH

and practice forgiveness for your
own peace of mind.

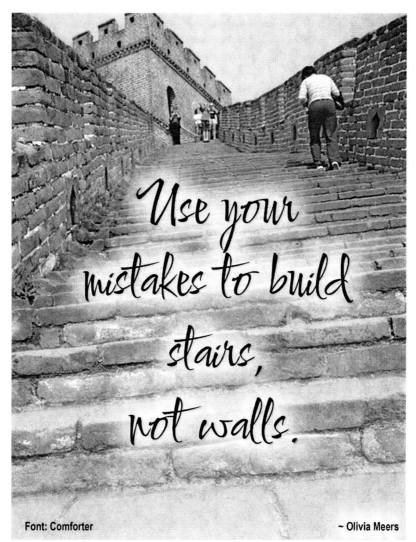

Font: Comforter   ~ Olivia Meers

We can either feel guilty about the mistakes we
make and surround ourselves in a wall of shame...
or we can look at our mistakes as a lesson in life
and learn from them. Mistakes help us grow..
if we let them.

Your intuition is a muscle. To develop it, you must listen.

Font: Akita

~ Phil Good

We were all born with intuition but, like a phyiscal muscle, if we don't use it and learn to trust it, we become unaware of its power to guide us. When your gut tells you something is right or wrong — that is your intuition kicking in. Listen to it!

Be someone who makes someone else...

look forward to tomorrow.

Font: Alisha

~ Author Unknown

If you can be the person who gives hope to another,
your own life will be filled with grace.
Help brighten someone's day and the world
will be brighter for both of you.

Your time has
come to shine!

Font: Aquarelle

~ Paul Simon
Bridge Over Troubled Waters

What you are going through now is opening you up to new possibilities, to a new way of "being" in the world. Indeed— it is your time to shine. As you let your light shine, you brighten the lives of everyone around you.

try
taking a
different
perspective.

Font: Heloran

~Brian McKnight

When something is troubling you, remember to ask your Higher Self to transform your thoughts so you can look at what is bothering you with a different perspective. Inner peace and happiness is your goal. Let go of any thought that doesn't support your goal.

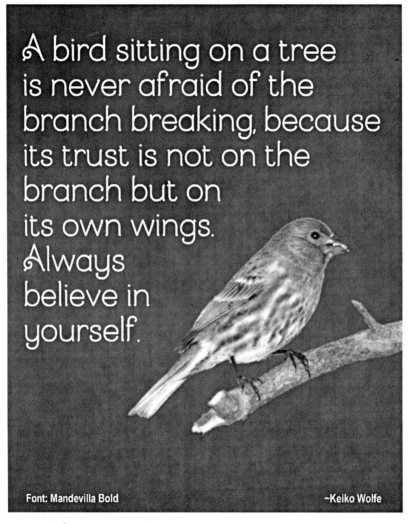

A bird sitting on a tree
is never afraid of the
branch breaking, because
its trust is not on the
branch but on
its own wings.
Always
believe in
yourself.

Font: Mandevilla Bold   ~Keiko Wolfe

The most important thing you can do for your
happiness is to believe in yourself.
You can create the life of your dreams but first you
must believe in yourself. Let go of any thought
that doesn't support your goal.

Whatever makes you feel bad, drop it. Whatever makes you feel good, keep it. Simple as that!

Font: Aquabella

~Graham Kean

This is a simple philosophy that makes sense. So often we find ourselves dwelling on the "bad" stuff, which only makes us feel miserable. So, drop the bad stuff while you focus on and keep the stuff that makes you feel good.

Let them judge you.
Let them misunderstand you.
Let them gossip about you.
Their opinions aren't your problem.
You stay kind, committed to love,
and free in your authenticity.
No matter what they do or say,
don't you dare doubt your worth
or the beauty of your truth.
Just keep on shining
like you do.

Font: Avilar

~ Scott Stabile

*Don't let those around you decide how you
feel about yourself.
Their opinions belong to them.... not you.
Only you can decide your worth and
you are a priceless treasure.*

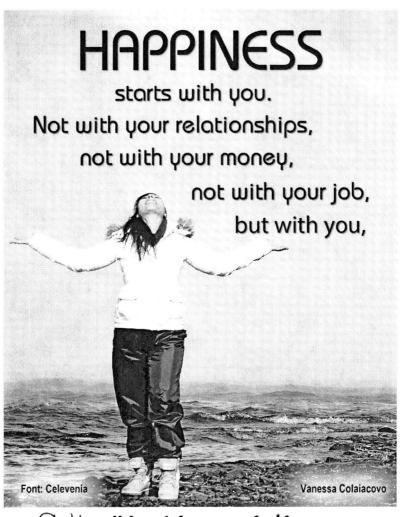

HAPPINESS
starts with you.
Not with your relationships,
not with your money,
not with your job,
but with you,

Font: Celevenia

Vanessa Colaiacovo

We've all heard the saying that "happiness is an inside job." The next step is to actually incorporate the truth of this saying into your belief system. Your happiness is solely dependent on how you feel about yourself, how you honor yourself, amd how you love yourself.

Font: Degreco

Author Unknown

I truly believe if you want to accomplish any goals in your life, you need to not only envision them, you also need to take action — small steps every day that lead toward your goal. You can accomplish whatever your heart desires through your vision and actions.

Dear beautiful you...
This is **your** life (your very own life).
Get to know **your** soul.
Dance **your** dance.
Sing **your** song.
Take charge of **your** story.
Love **your** day.
Let **your** heavy stuff go.
Embrace **your** blessings.
Kiss **your** beloveds.
Thank **your** everything.
See **your** place.
Forgive **your** mistakes. Forgive **your** enemies.
Drain **your** secrets of their poison.
Heal **your** pain. Find **your** tribe.
Rest **your** body. Share **your** talents.
Practice **your** passions. Find **your** bliss.
LIVE **YOUR** LIFE. LOVE **YOUR** LIFE.
Because the best years of your life will happen as
soon as you open your hands and your heart
to your happiness.

Font: Drawntastic   ~ Melody Ross

I encourage you to read and embrace the wise advice in this card because I truly believe the best years of your life lie ahead.

If you are determined to accomplish a goal,
make a plan,
break the plan into manageable steps
and work it everyday,
step by step.

Go confidently
in the direction
of your dreams.

Live the
life you've
imagined.

Fonts: Kayleight and Aileron   ~ Henry David Thoreau

*Never stop dreaming about the life you wish to
create for yourself and then be confident enough
in yourself to continue taking steps toward
living the life of your dreams.*

Fonts: Alterlight and Kon Tiki Enchanted ~ Based on Shakespeare

We all know how irritating it is to be around a phony -- someone who "puts on airs" to try to impress. The best advice is to always be real by being true to yourself. In that way you attract true friends who love you for who you are.

Font: Artstain   ~ Author Unknown

Achieving what we want in life requires that we break free from our limiting thoughts and take chances. That's what growth is all about. Whether we win or lose, the outcome is always on the plus side of growth.

Fonts: Blocked Artistry, Love Light, BioRhyme, Arial, Night Sky   ~ Susan Black

It is important to be brave enough and kind enough to yourself in order to be true to yourself. You, and only you, can discover and express your true calling in life.

How much of life do we miss by waiting to see the rainbow before thanking God that there is rain?

Font: Headmaster — Dieter F. Uchtdorf

They say that into each life some rain must fall as if rain is a bad thing. However, without rain, nothing grows. So if we can see those rainy periods of our lives as opportunities for growth, we can learn to appreciate the rain just as much as the rainbow.

MAKE *your own* LUCK

Fonts: Anagram & Amtenar   ~ Ernest Hemmingway to his son, Gregory

I truly believe that we actually do make our own luck by putting forth the effort of knowing what we want — being really clear about that — and then using the Law of Attraction to bring it into our lives.

Every day may
not be good.

but there is
something good
in every day.

Font: Bellagio

~ Alice Morese Earle

When we develop the habit of looking for
the good in every experience, it helps us get
through the rough times more easily.
Before you go to sleep each night, think of at
least one good thing that happened that day,
dwell on that as you fall asleep.

Interrupt Anxiety with Gratitude.

Font: Bernice

~ Danielle LaPorte

I have personally found that purposely entering into a state of gratitude completely lifts me out of any emotional turmoil I may be experiencing. When I feel worried or anxious, I simply start mentally listing everything in my life that I am grateful for... within minutes my mood has lifted.

I smile as I send you this card because
this is my 11th commandment.
Be true to yourself and
don't take shit from
anyone.

Train yourself to find the blessing in everything.

Font: Freshnap

~ Fiona Childs

Training yourself to find the blessing in every experience is the true path to living a happy life. Go on a treasure hunt for those jewels that are hiding in each experience and reap the happy rewards.

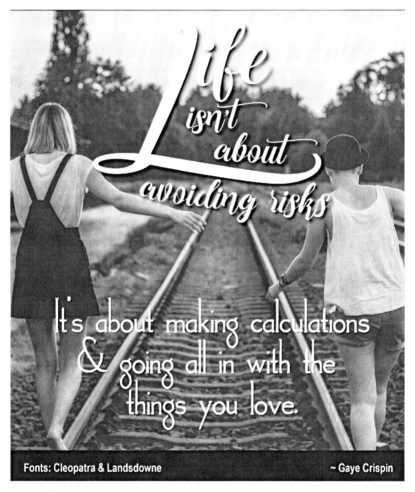

Fonts: Cleopatra & Landsdowne ~ Gaye Crispin

Never be afraid to try doing something you think you might love. If it doesn't work out -- you've learned a lesson and have grown from the experience. If it does work out, you've tapped into a joy you may have never known had you not been brave enough to give it a try.

Font: Golly Gosh   ~ Mom

Believing in yourself is the most important belief you can have in life. Without it you will never achieve your goals or live the life of your dreams.

Upon waking,
let your only thought be:

"THANK YOU!"

Font: Pathout ~ Sarah Ban Breathnach

*Starting each day in gratitude
sets the tone and intention for the day.
Sending you lots of love.*

I MAKE MY OWN

SUNSHINE!

Font: Flamingo ~ Alyssa Bonagura

You don't have to let other people influence how you feel. Decide to make your own sunshine and not only will you feel better -- you will lift the spirits of others -- win-win!

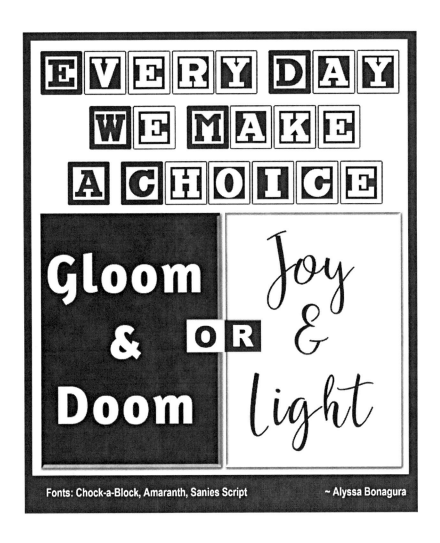

Focus on the "good stuff" whenever you can
and you will find that more and more
"good stuff" shows up in your life —
it is the "Law of Attraction" at work.

HAPPINESS IS A CHOICE

that requires effort at times.

Font: Bernice Regular and Times New Roman   ~ Aeschylus

Happiness, just like every other goal we strive to achieve, requires effort and dedication, especially in a relationship. The first step is to develop a loving relationship with yourself. Once you've achieved that, it is easier to find happiness in all your other relationships.

The best things in life...

aren't things.

Font: Nomura   ~ Art Buchwald

This saying emphasizes an important point
I know you have already discovered —
that the most important things
in life are not measured
by the things we possess, but by the love
we have of family and friends.

When you forgive

you don't change the past...

You change the future!

Fonts: Spotlight & Helvetica

~ Vincent Happy Mnisi

No one can change the past but we can change the future by forgiving not only those who may have hurt us but also forgiving ourselves for anything we may have done that has hurt another.
It is time to change the future...
It is time to forgive.

All that we behold

is full of

blessings.

Font: Stassi

~ William Wordsworth

Imagine how different the world would be if everyone developed the ability to see the blessings in every experience. Well, changing the world begins with each of us reaching a place within ourselves of gratitude for every experience. It takes some work, but it is well worth the effort.

FIND JOY IN THE JOURNEY.

Font: Sho-Card Caps
~ Thomas S. Monson

We don't always find ourselves where we want to be in life, but if we can shift our perception to understanding that life is a journey and that every experience along the way provides us with an opportunity to learn and to grow, we can then find joy in the journey.

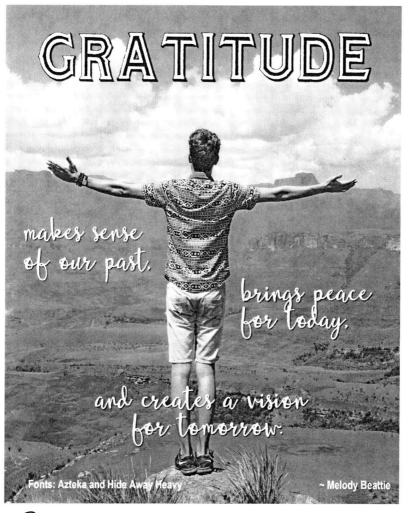

GRATITUDE

makes sense of our past,

brings peace for today,

and creates a vision for tomorrow.

Fonts: Azteka and Hide Away Heavy

~ Melody Beattie

One of the most effective ways to reach a state of inner peace is to put yourself into a state of gratitude. Instead of being upset about a situation, try being grateful for the lesson it is teaching you and for the opportunity to do things differently the next time.

Create a life that feels GREAT on the inside and doesn't just look good on the outside.

Font: Carlington

~ Heather McClosky Beck

I feel this is a really important lesson. If we don't feel good on the inside, it doesn't matter how much money or fame we have, we will not feel happy or fulfilled.

HAPPINESS

SOME PURSUE IT...

others

CREATE IT!

Fonts: Chaos Becker2, Radio Days, LS Leaves ~ Ralph Walso Emerson

I am a firm believer that in order to find
happiness in life we need to create it
and we do that through love --
the love of yourself,
the love of your family and friends,
the love of your work in the world.

GIVING

is the best way

to be

FULFILLED.

Fonts: Cleaver's Juvenia & Synthesia

~ Sean McCabe

I am sure that everyday you are in contact with someone who is going through a rough time. By being there to help someone weather their own storm, you will bring blessings upon yourself.

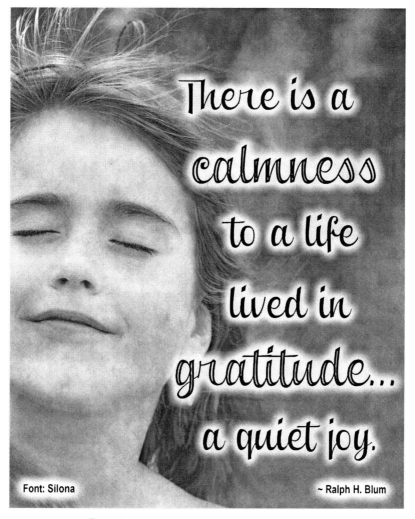

There is a
calmness
to a life
lived in
gratitude...
a quiet joy.

Font: Silona

~ Ralph H. Blum

Whenever you feel yourself
becoming overwhelmed with life, take
the time to start focusing on your
many blessings and in that way you can
shift into the quiet joy of gratitude.

When you help
someone up a hill...

you get that much closer
to the top, yourself!

Font: Vandella   ~ Mary Engelgreit

*Helping others and doing good deeds
is a great way to lift your own spirits.
Whatever you give out always
comes back to you in
countless ways.*

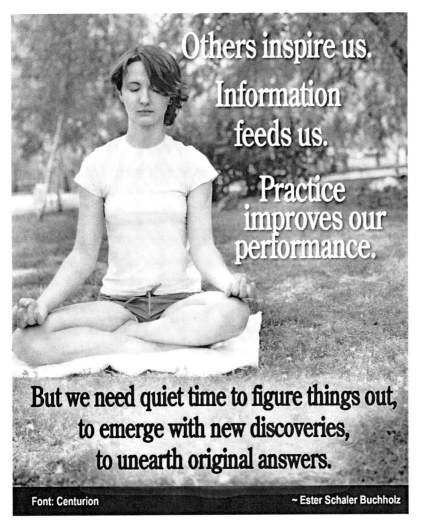

Others inspire us.
Information feeds us.
Practice improves our performance.

But we need quiet time to figure things out,
to emerge with new discoveries,
to unearth original answers.

Font: Centurion   ~ Ester Schaler Buchholz

*It is a good practice to build "alone time"
into your life. It is not always easy to do,
but it is one of the most important things
you can do for yourself.*

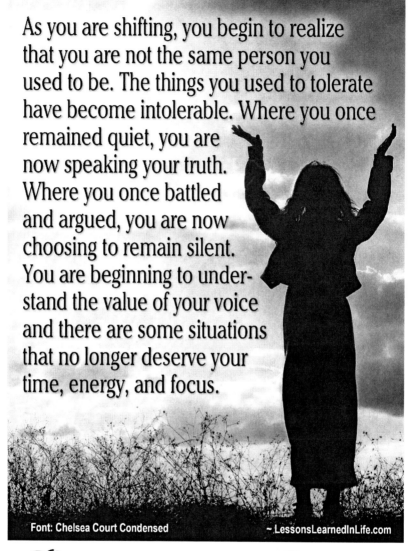

As you are shifting, you begin to realize that you are not the same person you used to be. The things you used to tolerate have become intolerable. Where you once remained quiet, you are now speaking your truth. Where you once battled and argued, you are now choosing to remain silent. You are beginning to under-stand the value of your voice and there are some situations that no longer deserve your time, energy, and focus.

Font: Chelsea Court Condensed   ~ LessonsLearnedInLife.com

This is an important message. You are not the same person you were six months ago. Value the changes you are going through and the person you are becoming.

Fonts: Spotlight & Night Sky

~ John 9:5

Never hide your inner light and no matter where you find yourself in life — let your light shine.

Soon, when all is well, you're going to look back on this period of your life and be so glad that you never gave up!

Font: Hide Away

~ Brittany Burgunder

I know you are already beginning to realize that this journey is helping you to become a stronger, wiser woman. It is a major turning point in your life. I'm so proud of you!

I've really grown to appreciate the value of meditation. Every creative idea I've ever had has come out of the my meditation practice. There are many ways to meditate -- Take time to explore a few different approaches to meditation and choose one that works for you.

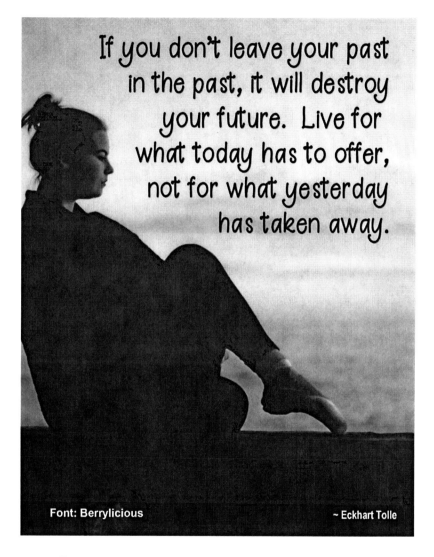

If you don't leave your past in the past, it will destroy your future. Live for what today has to offer, not for what yesterday has taken away.

Font: Berrylicious

~ Eckhart Tolle

It is so important to learn from your past, allow its lessons to inform you, and then move on to a brighter tomorrow.

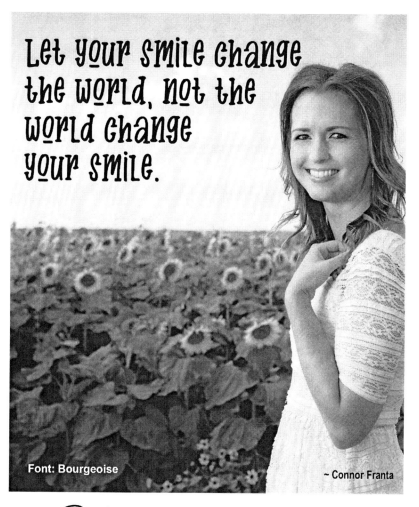

Let your smile change the world, not the world change your smile.

Font: Bourgeoise

~ Connor Franta

Don't let the world or your present circumstances take away your ability to be happy. Smile through it and you will make yourself and everyone around you feel lighter and brighter. Shine on...

When she transformed
into a butterfly

the caterpillars spoke not of her
beauty, but of her weirdness.

They wanted her to change back
into what she always
had been.

But she had
WINGS!

Font: Horace   ~ Dean Jackson

*Think of this time as your cocoon stage.
Soon you will emerge as a new person ready
to spread your wings and fly away home!*

The future belongs to those who believe in the beauty of their DREAMS.

Font: Balgis

~ Eleanor Roosevelt

Never stop believing that you can achieve the life of your dreams.
Dream BIG!

LIFE won't SPARKLE unless YOU do.

Fonts: By Starlight & Thirteenth Alt3   ~ Author Unknown

Never lose your sparkle...
you were born to shine!

Your hardest times often lead to the greatest moments of your life. Keep the faith.

It will all be worth it in the end.

Font: Brentford   ~ Roy Bennett

I know what you are going through is not easy. But I have faith that you will look back on this experience with gratitude knowing that it was instrumental in setting your life's path in a new direction of strength and personal empowerment.
Keep the faith!

Font: Calligraphy Script   ~ William Arthur Ward

I've learned that I can't depend on someone else to make me happy — happiness comes from my own self-worth. Once I learned to love myself, my world changed and I began to attract people into my life who validated what I was feeling inside — love and happiness.

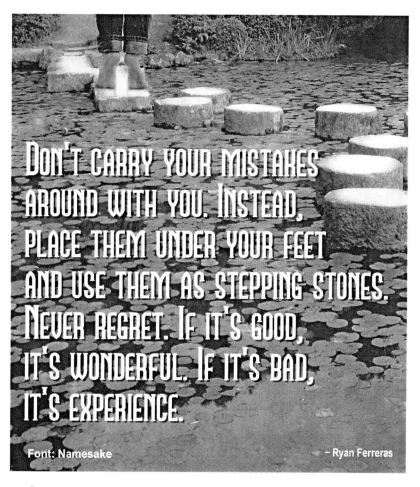

DON'T CARRY YOUR MISTAKES AROUND WITH YOU. INSTEAD, PLACE THEM UNDER YOUR FEET AND USE THEM AS STEPPING STONES. NEVER REGRET. IF IT'S GOOD, IT'S WONDERFUL. IF IT'S BAD, IT'S EXPERIENCE.

Font: Namesake

~ Ryan Ferreras

We all make mistakes —that is one way we learn to navigate life. It is important, however, to never let your mistakes define your opinion of yourself.
Think of mistakes as lessons that help guide you toward making better choices.

Font: Dark Manga   ~ Mom

It is important to remember that you are a warrior! So whenever you feel down, summon your inner warrior to raise you up and meet your challenges bravely and with confidence.

Being happy doesn't mean everything is perfect.

It means you've decided to look beyond the imperfections.

Font: Anjanie

~ Gerard Way

My prayer for you is that once you have completed this phase of your journey, you will find true happiness.

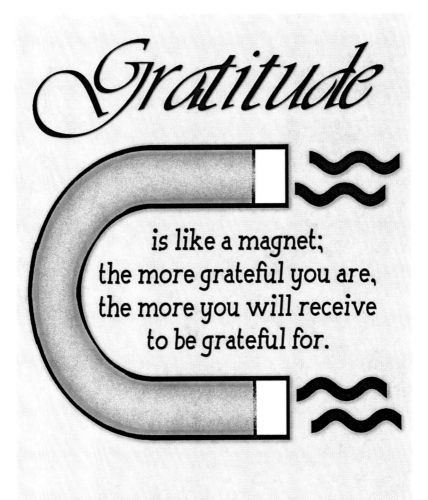

Gratitude

is like a magnet;
the more grateful you are,
the more you will receive
to be grateful for.

Fonts: Astrania & Dunkel Meister   ~ Iyanla Vanzant

*A great way to feel happier is to make
a mental list of everything you are
grateful for, as you focus on gratefulness,
you automatically lift your spirits.*

It is really important to avoid spending time with negative people. They are bad for your physical, psychological and spiritual health as they consume your valuable time with their dramas and bring your energy down.

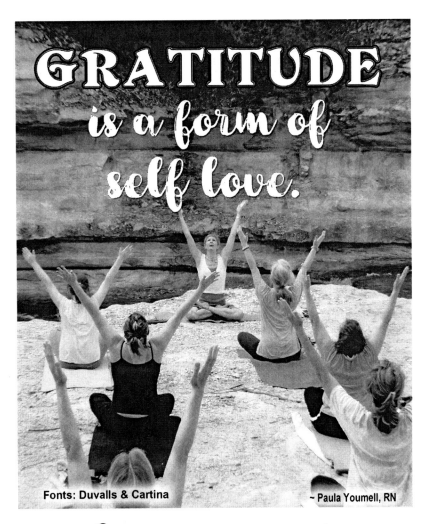

GRATITUDE is a form of self love.

Fonts: Duvalls & Cartina   ~ Paula Youmell, RN

Self love begins with gratitude.
How do I teach people the Lighten Up
process? I tell them to spend 5 minutes each
day thanking every part of their bodies.
This is HOW self love begins.

When you make a choice, you change the future.

THIS WAY

THAT WAY

Fonts: Colleen   ~ Deepak Chopra

Every time we make a choice, we change the future. This is a powerful concept to ponder. Since we are continually creating our future by the choices we make, it is imperative that we choose wisely!

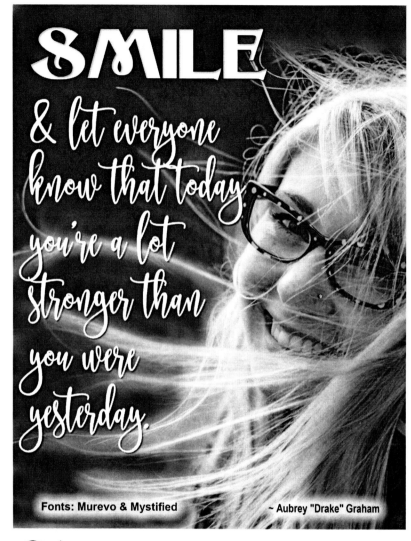

SMILE

& let everyone know that today you're a lot stronger than you were yesterday.

Fonts: Murevo & Mystified

~ Aubrey "Drake" Graham

When we smile we not only make ourselves feel better, we lighten our environment and help those around us to also feel better. Keep smiling.

Take it day
by day and
be grateful
for every
breath.

FROM PARIS

Fonts: Memotype

~ Positive Outlook Quote

When we consciously put ourselves into a state of gratitude every day, our life noticeably improves as we begin to attract more and more goodness into our lives.

If you don't like something, change it.

If you can't change it, change the way you think about it.

Fonts: Maphylia

~ Mary Engelbreit

You are definitely in the process of a huge change that is going to enable you to lead a happier, more fulfilling life. I'm so very proud of you!

No one ever injured their eyesight

by looking on the bright side.

Font: Muchaka   ~ Author Unknown

When things aren't going your way, it's easy to dwell on the negative, and by doing that you attract more negativity. That's why it's really important to transform your negative thoughts and enhance your positive thoughts by looking on the the bright side.

Gratitude unlocks the fullness of life. It turns what we have into enough, and more. It turns denial into acceptance, chaos to order, confusion to clarity. It can turn a meal into a feast, a house into a home, a stranger into a friend.

Gratitude makes sense of our past, bring peace for today, and creates a vision for tomorrow.

Fonts: ChromaScript   **~ Melody Beattie**

I love this quote that "Gratitude makes sense of our past, brings peace for today, and creates a (positive) vision for tomorrow." When we look at our past and contemplate the positive benefits (gifts) we've received from every experience we can truly be grateful for our past and make peace with it.

(Note: I added "positive" to the quote).

I love the ones who stay in my life and make me happier.

I also love the ones who left my life and made me stronger!

Fonts: Shailena

~ Author Unknown

This is a great and positive way to view those people in our lives who we dislike for one reason or another. They pushed our buttons and made us stronger! They served their purpose. Hooray!

Never be defined by your past. It was just a lesson... not a life sentence.

Font: Tervana

~ Karen Salmansohn

It is important to learn from our past mistakes so that we can make life adjustments to set a new life course—one that takes all our lessons learned, leads us to make wise decisions and thus create a happier, more fulfilling life.

Give
every
day the
chance
to
become
the
most
beautiful
of your
life.

~ Mark Twain

No matter what we are going through, there are things in our lives for which we can be grateful. Focus on those things and create your own sunshine. By so doing, you can make each day beautiful.
It us not always easy,
but it's worth the effort.

YOU ARE ALLOWED
to terminate toxic relationships.

YOU ARE ALLOWED
to walk away from people who hurt you.

YOU ARE ALLOWED
to be angry and selfish and unforgiving.

YOU DON'T OWE ANYONE AN EXPLANATION
for taking care of yourself.

Fonts: Ansley Display & Allura   ~ Steve Maraboli

This is another great reminder about loving yourself enough to let go of everything toxic in your life.

And the day came when the risk to remain tight in the bud was more painful than the risk to blossom.

Font: Magnificent

~ Anais Nin

I feel that one of the things you are learning on this journey is to open up to your feelings and express them — the first steps to blossoming into personal empowerment. I'm so proud of you!

When you get out of bed each morning
make a resolution that no matter what
the day may bring, you will look for
and acknowledge all the
hidden joys you can uncover.

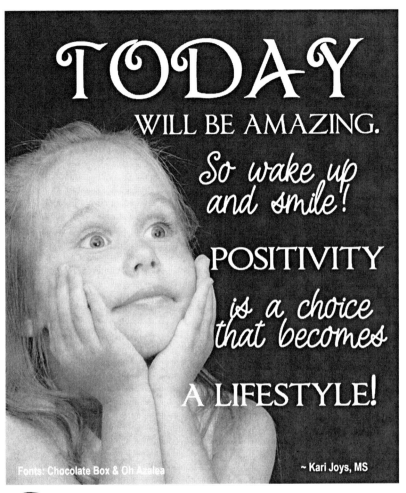

TODAY WILL BE AMAZING. So wake up and smile! POSITIVITY is a choice that becomes A LIFESTYLE!

Fonts: Chocolate Box & Oh Azalea

~ Kari Joys, MS

I know it is not easy to always keep a positive attitude. What is definitely good to remember, however, is that deciding whether or not to be positive is a choice you have the power to make. Keep choosing to put on a happy face. You are a strong woman and you have the strength to choose to be positive.

You will find that it is necessary to let things go. simply for the reason that they are heavy.

Font: Hey Girl Regular

~ C. Joybell

I know what you are going through right now is not easy. The only real thing you have control over is your thoughts. Use the Free Yourself process and the Serenity Prayer to help get you through this challenging time.

There are no shortcuts to anywhere worth going.

Font: Roman Antique

~ Beverly Sills

You are on an amazing (and difficult) journey now of self-discovery and personal empowerment. Each step you take on this journey is making you stronger and more resilient. Don't give up hope.
It will all be worth it.

Life can only be understood backwards,

but must be lived forward.

Font: Cornelia

~ Soren Kierkegaard

We don't always understand why certain challenges and experiences show up in our lives. One thing I have learned, however, is that each experience has, in some way, helped me grow, if I focus on the gift it gave me and let go of any negative thoughts about it.

The important thing is not to get stuck — keep moving forward.

Just when the caterpillar thought the world was over,

it became a butterfly.

Font: Balqis

~ Chuang Tzu

Right now you are in a cocoon that is helping you become stronger and emerge ready to experience life in a new and more empowered way. Trust the process and keep your eye on the prize — a healthy, fulfilling life.

We can complain because rose bushes have thorns.

or rejoice because thorn bushes have roses.

Font: Bolton Bold

~ Abraham Lincoln

Every life experience, no matter how painful, has a gift. In fact, the most painful experiences often give us our greatest gifts.
As you go through this challenging time, keep asking yourself what positive lessons can I learn from this.
It will help you shift your attitude.

Imagine with all your mind.
Believe with all your heart.
Achieve with all your might.

Fonts: Abraham & Almondia

~ Evan Carmichael

The first step in reaching any goal is to use your power of imagination and visualize what it will feel like when you've achieved your goal. The next step is to believe that you can accomplish it and transform any thoughts that you can't. The last step is to do the work of achieving your goal — if you need to take a class or learn a new skill, or simply carve out the time to do it.

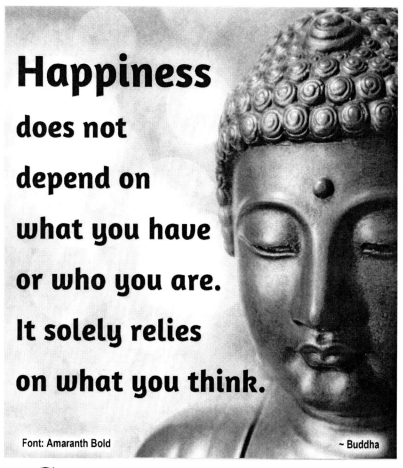

Happiness does not depend on what you have or who you are. It solely relies on what you think.

Font: Amaranth Bold

~ Buddha

You will probably never reach a state of happiness in your current situation, but what you can do is visualize how happy you will be when you come through this challenging time as a stronger and more empowered woman. Keep transforming all the negative thoughts. You will reach your goal.

Ego says: "Once everything
falls into place,
I will find peace."

Spirit says: "Find peace
and everything
will fall into place."

Font: Lanturna ~ Mariane Williamson

When you can reach a state of peace with your current situation, everything will start falling into place. To reach that state of peace you need to pay attention to your thoughts. Ask to have the negative ones transformed and add positive affirmations to your daily ritual.

Font: Malibu Regular

~ Otis Redding "My Girl" Lyrics

Your life probably seems pretty cloudy right now, so it is important for you to remember that you can make your own sunshine. You do that through your thoughts. Keep thinking sunny thoughts and the clouds will begin to dissipate.

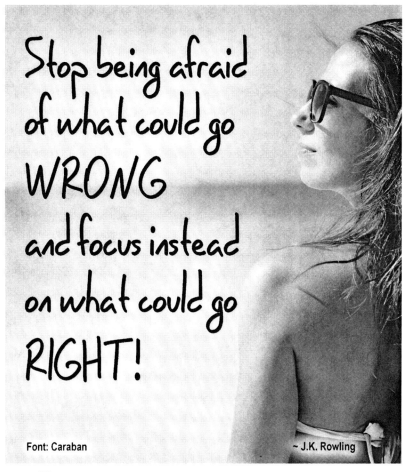

Stop being afraid
of what could go
WRONG
and focus instead
on what could go
RIGHT!

Font: Caraban   ~ J.K. Rowling

It is so important to focus your attention
on what you want to achieve and
visualize, visualize, visualize it coming true —
see everything falling into place.
When you worry about what could go wrong
— you will attract that. Keep your positive
vision front and center in your mind.

The primary cause of unhappiness is never the situation but your thoughts about it.

Font: Claritty

~ Eckhart Tolle

Even though you are going through a really challenging time right now, if you are willing to critically examine your thoughts about your situation and ask to have any negative thoughts transformed, it will help you get through this ordeal more easily.

I can't change the world, but I can change the world in me.

Font: Elf Tale

~ Bono

It is important to understand the impact we have on the world when we change ourselves in positive ways. Learn to love and forgive yourself and it will have a ripple effect in the world.

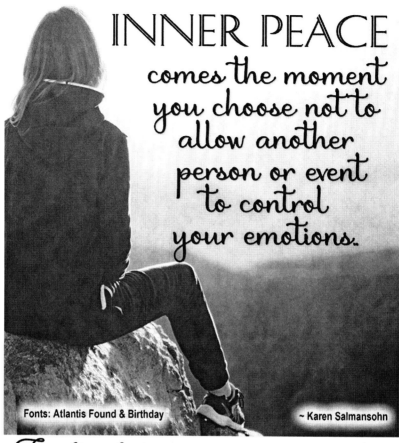

INNER PEACE
comes the moment
you choose not to
allow another
person or event
to control
your emotions.

Fonts: Atlantis Found & Birthday ~ Karen Salmansohn

To achieve lasting inner peace you must first understand that feeling at peace is a choice. It begins with monitoring your thoughts about yourself and your perceived situation, transforming any negative thoughts and making the choice to love yourself unconditionally. Once you love yourself, no person or event can disrupt your inner peace.

Stress is the alarm clock that lets you know you've attached to something...

YIKES
UH-OH   HELP
YUCK   OH NO
UGH   WHY ME
PHEW   GEEZ
WOW   YOW
OH SHIT

NOT TRUE FOR YOU!

Font: Carval Bold   ~ Byron Katie

Whenever you are feeling stressed-out, it is important to identify the underlying thoughts. In that way you can take positive action to physically change the situation that is causing the stress, or transform the thoughts by doing the Free Yourself process.

As you learn to love yourself, you also
learn how important it is to be yourself.
You will then attract people into
your life who resonate with
and compliment your energy.

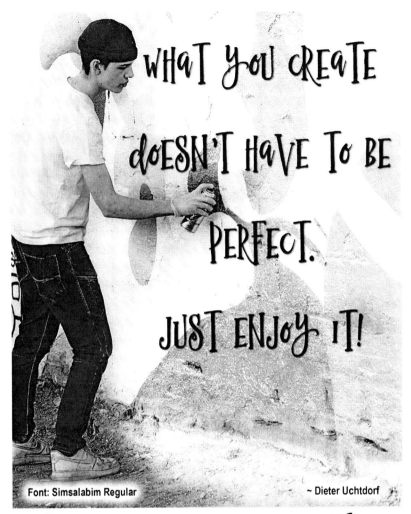

WHAT YOU CREATE

DOESN'T HAVE TO BE

PERFECT.

JUST ENJOY IT!

Font: Simsalabim Regular

~ Dieter Uchtdorf

This is an important lesson to learn. The art of creation is a journey and the most important aspect of the journey is that we enjoy it. When we step out of joy, it is a message to us that we need to adjust our compass and go in a different direction.

It is your reaction to adversity,
not the adversity itself,
that determines how
your life's story
will develop.

Font: Cavorting

~ Dieter Uchtdorf

This is a good reminder that how we react to situations in our lives determines our happiness level. It is important to learn to step away when necessary.

Please don't hide your inner AWESOME... The world needs it!

Font: Aivengo

~ Katrina Mayer

Being awesome is about being your greatest self and putting yourself and what you have to offer out into the world. I encourage you to move forward making a positive difference in your life and the lives of others.

I've always believed you are awesome — the trick is for you to believe it!

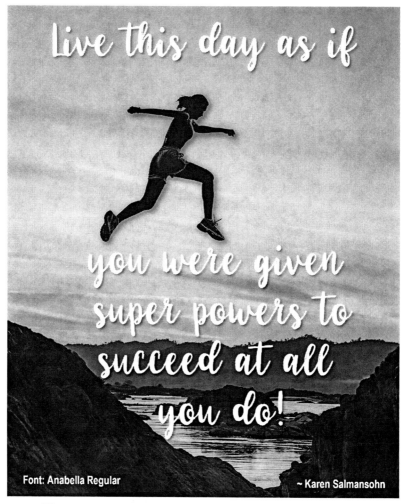

Imagine how differently we'd all live our lives if we believed we had super powers to succeed at everything we want to accomplish. The first step, of course, is believing in ourselves. My message to you is to know you are loved and I believe in you!

Wherever life plants you,
bloom with grace.

Font: Israquella   ~ French Proverb

Sometimes it takes a little while to bloom
when life plants you in a difficult or
challenging situation, but with the right
attitude it's always possible.
I am so proud of how you are blossoming
and I know you will continue to bloom!

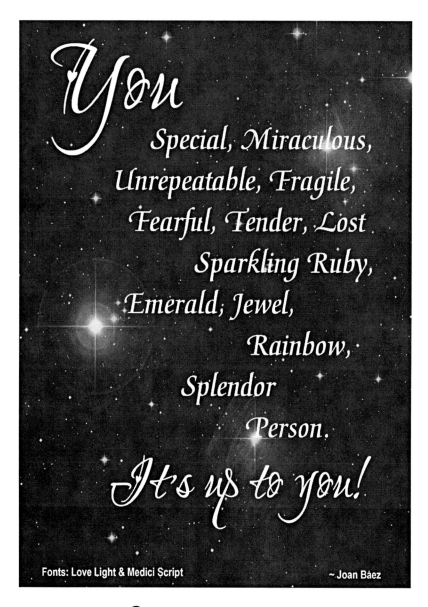

You
Special, Miraculous,
Unrepeatable, Fragile,
Fearful, Tender, Lost
Sparkling Ruby,
Emerald, Jewel,
Rainbow,
Splendor
Person.
It's up to you!

Fonts: Love Light & Medici Script   ~ Joan Báez

*Simply a reminder of
just how amazing you are!*

Free Yourself from Fear

Free Yourself from Fear is a spiritual process of personal empowerment that was inspired in 1995 during one of Carol's daily meditations with *A Course in Miracles*. After using it successfully on herself, she began sharing it with her friends and clients. Everyone she worked with began to experience positive life changes as they used the process to transform their negative and limiting thoughts. You can read what makes the Free Yourself process unique at <www.freeyourselffromfear.com/about>

Lighten Up

This five minute-a-day process will bring you into a state of unconditional love of yourself. Carol has sold over 20,000 Lighten Up recordings and more than 5000 people have experienced the magic of her workshops. Find out more at <openheartpress.com/products/lighten-up-cd>

COMING SOON!
Know Your Are Loved Greeting Cards

These greeting cards are designed specifically to be sent to loved ones who are in a residential rehab facility or prison to encourage and support them lovingly through their challenging journey. They will soon be available through Open Heart Press. For more information about the greeting cards as well as other Know You Are Loved products, visit our website at: **KnowYouAreLoved.info**. Be sure to subscribe to our mailing list if you would like to be informed about when the greeting cards will be available.

About the Author

Carol Hansen Grey is an author, empowerment coach and graphic designer. She runs a publishing company (Open Heart Press) with her husband, Victor Grey. She believes that self-love and personal empowerment are keys to creating world peace. So her passion is to create a world of harmony and peace by helping people love and empower themselves. She does this through her personal empowerment coaching sessions, her CDs, the books she writes, the greeting cards she designs and the websites she creates.

Other Books by Carol

Simple Healing Tools on the Path to Personal Empowerment and Inner Peace (available on Amazon in paperback & ebook)

How Do I Love Myself? Learn a Magical 5 Minute-a-Day Process (ebook available on Amazon)

How Do I Create Peace Within Myself and in the World? (ebook available on Amazon)

You can read more about Carol on her various websites:
CarolHansenGrey.com, FreeYourselfFromFear.com,
SimpleHealingTools.com, OpenHeart.com,
PersonalEmpowermentPath.com,
KnowYouAreLoved.info and
OpenHeartEnterprises.com

Some examples of the envelopes Carol created and sent to her daughter while she was in rehab can be found at carolhansengrey.com/inspiration/envelopes.html

CPSIA information can be obtained
at www.ICGtesting.com
Printed in the USA
FSOW02n1712241117
41500FS